FRE
ON THE FAULT LINE

LILIJA VALIS

outskirts press
Denver, Colorado

Outskirts Press, Inc.
http://www.outskirtspress.com

ISBN: 978-1-4327-7619-0

Library of Congress Control Number: 2011933615

PRINTED IN THE UNITED STATES OF AMERICA

This book is dedicated to people who seek to free themselves politically, socially, or spiritually without subjugating others to their inevitably errant will.

The love of freedom is a mysterious thing, connected to the love of one's family, community, and the land of one's ancestors, and to something bigger still, a loyalty to the Spirit within all life that seeks to flourish.

To Ron –

a seeker of the light
in snow-purified mountains,
a builder of community
through generosity of Spirit
and goodness in action –
without which freedom
cannot leave the cave.

Lilija Valis
March 2012

Contents

PREFACE i

THE WORD FREEDOM iii

READ THE FINE PRINT

FREEDOM 1
UNINVITED GUESTS 2
I DON'T LIKE YOU 6
SPACE 10
RUNNING OUT OF SYMPATHY 11
THE DENIERS 15
POLITICS 17
LIFE IN THE SKY 19
RENTAL AGREEMENT 20
THOUGHTS 23
PUSHING BACK 25
A HARMONIOUS SOCIETY 26
WHAT WE DO 28
CRISSCROSSING 29
CERTAINTY 30
GRAY PLACE 31
TRAFFIC 32
A LIFE 33
SAD STORY 34
UP TO YOU 35
ACID 36
CAGED 37
ELIZABETH I, AFTER THERAPY 39

THE AGE OF TALKERS 42
PRISON 46
THE KEY 48
CHANGE 49
ENEMY 50
HATE IS A FULL-TIME JOB 52
NO ESCAPE 54
NO LIMITS 55
EDUCATION 56
DON'T DO IT 57
MOCK EXECUTION 58

ONE INVITATION IS ALL YOU GET
SAFETY 61
STOP SIGN 62
WALLS 63
INVITATION 64
SYMPATHY 66
HOME 67
VANCOUVER EVENING 68
MARRIAGE 69
POSTJUDICE 70
EVERYTHING IS TEMPORARY 72
CONFESSIONS OF A DO-GOODER 73
NO BLAME 74
VIRUS 75
QUALITY 77
CAN'T HELP IT 79
IN THE DRIVER'S SEAT 80
NOT TRUE 82
FINAL SOLUTION 83

ONE 84
DON'T ASK 85
SILENT MOVIE 86
THE PLEDGE 87
IF 88
OFF ENDS 90
LIGHT 91
BEWARE 92
RESTLESS 93
RING OF FIRE 94
THE CHOSEN 97
EVERYDAY THINGS 100
A TOAST 101
TRAVEL ADVICE 102
A CHANCE 103

ACKNOWLEDGMENTS 105

PREFACE

I have always aspired to a more spacious form
that would be free from the claims of poetry or prose

The purpose of poetry is to remind us
how difficult it is to remain just one person,
for our house is open, there are no keys in the doors,
and invisible guests come in and out at will.

— Czeslaw Milosz, *Ars Poetica?*

THE WORD FREEDOM

(Compiled from The Shorter Oxford English Dictionary on Historical Principles and the Oxford Canadian, and Webster's dictionaries.)

FREE: from Old English *freo*
Indo-European *prijos*
Sanskrit *prijas,* meaning dear
and *pri – to love*
primary meaning: dear

not subject as a slave to a master
released from slavery or imprisonment
not in bondage or under control of another

existing under a government that is not despotic

permitted to go anywhere
capable of movement
unrestricted, unobstructed

free from arbitrary control or fate
released from ties, obligations, pressure

acting of one's own will or choice
power of self
independent of fate or necessity
not determined from without

available without charge

innocent, acquitted (1602)

frank, bold

open, spontaneous

generous, noble (1604)

DOM: from Latin *domus (Dei)*
house of God

Old English suffix: jurisdiction, domain, realm.

READ THE FINE PRINT

FREEDOM

What I don't have enough of
but others have too much

what comes attached to things
everyone wants to avoid

what draws those who lack it
to seize too much and wreck it

what is rejected when possessed
and sought after when lost

what looks promising on paper
but gets bloodied in the streets

what songs are made of
and jails filled with

what requires laws for others
but only advice for me.

UNINVITED GUESTS

You came to liberate us.
We didn't remember complaining
to you. We resisted your coming

but you had more tanks.
You dropped bombs on our homes,
our doors opened.

You pointed your guns at us
and promised us happiness:
equality under the gun.

We had a university far older
than any in your vast land
but you had things to teach us.

To make us worthy of new things
you took away our old ones.

You said the piano had to go
to your home.
Out went our icons and books,
the ancient amber jewelry,
fashionable dresses.

People learned to hide
anything of value
when they saw you coming.

But there was no end
to what you claimed
we did not need;
no end to what you wanted.

You demanded our loyalty
but we had at least five thousand years
of resistance written into our DNA.

You dragged us away
from the land of our songs.
You crowded us into cattle trains
to your icy north
for the work none of you
wanted to do.
You kept the rewards.

When at last we pushed you out
two generations later
your spirit remained in the things
you left for us:
tacky art
high-rise slums
hard liquor distilleries in every town
toilets that refuse to flush
empty shops
queues
faces that turn away.

In the center of our main city
is an old stone building

you had turned into
an interrogation center:
the information you extracted
dripped with blood.

We are getting rid of your things.
We like to choose our own.
We will keep your footprint
to remind us
where not to go.

Outside one town
forty thousand crosses crowd a hill.
They lean into each other
as if for comfort,
the small ones carried by the large,
artisan or home-made,
intricately wrought,
amber-encrusted,
rosary-draped,
inscribed with a few words,
each cross a life that ended
against the barbed wire
of your happiness.

You kept pulling the crosses down
and burning them.
We kept replacing them in the night.

If you don't want to see grief,
don't come without an invitation.

While you're waiting,
don't worry about
your dead in our cemeteries.
The women who visit
place flowers on the graves
of both friend and enemy.
All equal in death, we say.

I DON'T LIKE YOU

(Dedicated to those who love humanity and have big plans for it.)

I don't like you
but I leave you alone.

You say you love me
yet you want to rehabilitate me.

Of course, you mean
people in general
and I'm a people
though in particular.

I will listen to what you say.
If I don't like your words,
I may give you some of mine
or I may not
but I will not accuse you of heresy.

The punishment for heresy
is death
of one sort or another.

You love me,
so you say,
yet you make my thoughts
a crime.
You forbid me to defend myself
against people who harm me.

If you spare my life,
I still lose.
I have to change my name
so I can sweep floors somewhere,
but you will still find me.

I don't like the way you love,
why you hate,
how you pray,
even the way you dress.

But I'm cool.
I don't stand in your way.

You want to create a paradise
on this unstable earth
and you want me in it,
but you demand I hide my face.
You throw a shadow on my path.

You use elaborate systems,
made of nails and blades,
to give you the right-of-way
into my life.

You say God and economics
demand this.

You have a history
I don't like.
You loved my country so much
you wanted it different,
so you built prisons.

You want happiness for all,
that's what you said,
then sent those who resisted
to die of starvation and cold
                              and bullets
digging your mines
to make you happy.

I don't like you.
You always want what's best for others.
You speak for us
and decide what we want.
You choose who will live with us,
work with us,
who will cut us
when we're in pain.

You tell us who we must like
and who deserves hate.
You must know hate is a trap.
So who are you trapping:
the haters or the hated?

We fear telling what we see.
We pretend to see what is not.

Your happiness is not my happiness.
You're welcome to yours.
Leave me to my misery.
My misery is my happiness.
You don't like my happiness.
Freedom makes some people miserable.
Not me.

I don't like your paradise.
Don't push me into it.
Even if you force me to clap and cheer
at your parade,
you can't rehabilitate me.

I don't like you,
but changing you
hasn't caught my interest.

You love me,
so you say,
and you plot my life.

Oh, if only you didn't love me so much!

I don't like you.
Leave me alone.

SPACE

Freedom is the space,
small but adjustable,
in a family, a nation,
set in the present, within a past,
lit by the promise of a future
on this unpredictable,
but achingly beautiful planet,
stalked by death, with
its armies of destruction.

RUNNING OUT OF SYMPATHY

I joined others
to dismantle the barriers
that kept you out.
You wanted to end
your history of separation.

My own family had fled
barbed wire. I recognized
our connection.

With others, I threw
my life across the mud
so you could cross.

When you got what you wanted,
what you wanted increased.

Like other sympathizers
I fed you excuses you could use.

You wiped your boots
on the unprotected.
You looked at your footprint
on my face and laughed.

Where you saw weakness,
you took what you coveted
and destroyed what you
couldn't carry.

Authority was on your side.
You could do no wrong.
This made your wrongs bolder.

Your right-of-way, you said,
went through my life.

You made my home
what you fled from.

You moved into the neighborhood
where my father lived.
He was elderly and frail.
On his way to the local store
he walked past you,
hanging out in the street,
young and strong,
the three of you.
You hurled sharp words at him.
He kept his eyes on the ground
but it wasn't enough.
You kicked and beat him,
and took what you found
of his small pension.

"Respect," you ordered
as you pushed me
off the sidewalk
after a riot.

You used endless grievances
from the past to build
prisons for strangers.

You wrote poetry
about the ways you'd like
to kill me and those like me
and you taught it to our children.

You blamed others when
the more daring among you
shot a passer-by
or poured gasoline on a stranger
from another country,
and lit a match.

You find pleasure
in putting others
where you did not like to be.

I'm running out of sympathy.
Thanks for releasing me.
Sympathy, past a certain point,
can maim, you and me.

You finished my education.
The cost was a surprise.
I paid only a portion;
others paid the rest.
You are my PhD
in laws governing life.

I learned a new language;
don't need a translator anymore.

The protected are disadvantaged.
Knowledge is shelter.

THE DENIERS

If you deny
what I assert
I will hunt you down

even though
I don't know you,
you don't know me,
and neither of us
witnessed what I assert
and you deny.

All I know about you is
you're not one of us.

I will call you names,
disgrace you,
take your money
and your job,
kick you out
of your community,
isolate you in prison.

One way or another
I will silence you
and anyone else
thinking of denying.

I will defend
to the death
my right to deny you
any opportunity to deny
what I assert.

POLITICS

Politics is not politics.

It's what you think of me
and how I see you;

it's family and the stranger;
it's who will do the work
and who will get the reward;

it's how we decide
who owns what and
who the thieves are;

it's how we act when
we see a child broken
from a beating, or a dog
chained and starved;

it's marriage and divorce
and what we teach our children;

it's what we do when floods
carry away our lives,
when fire surrounds us.

No, politics is not politics;
it's you and me

and how we decide
to live together;

it's love and hate
and everything in between.

LIFE IN THE SKY

Caging a bird
is not a political act.
Destroying its life in the sky
is a curse on life,
and that moves it
into the spiritual realm.

RENTAL AGREEMENT

I understand the concept:
If you want something
you have to offer what is asked
                    in exchange.
You could try to negotiate;
the other party doesn't have to.

If you want money
to buy more freedom,
you have to rent yourself out,
          losing some freedom.

You hope the freedom
you'll buy eventually
will be more than you will lose now.

I worked for the government.
My profession was helping.
Everyone spoke
from the same script.
Sometimes I fell off the page.

I was sent to teamwork classes.
My mind had too much free space.
They were certain they had rented
                    all the space.
I thought I had rented out
only a section.

Ideas they claimed did not fit in
were wandering through my mind
disturbing their beliefs.

People walked into our program
seeking help. They left crawling.
Then they stopped leaving home.
They were told
        they would always need us.

We would always be paid
for being needed.
As the number of people
needing us increased,
so did the money
taken from people
who did not need us.

My office window faced
the back of a row of cars.
Their emissions mixed
with the office air.

There were people
who put aside their troubles
                    to say to me,
"How can you work here?
You're breathing air that
people commit suicide with."

Money makes demands
however you get it.
But doesn't everything?
And everybody?
Freedom makes demands.

The concept is simple
but the rental agreement is not.

Read the fine print:
It could be a bill of sale.

THOUGHTS

They accused you of thinking
your thoughts.
They ordered theirs to take over
but you barred their entrance.
Their thoughts were in uniform
and you knew they would not allow
yours to travel freely.

They hauled you
in front of a tribunal.
They presented evidence
you were thinking
not their thoughts.

The court room was hushed.
Your lawyer presented evidence
you did not think.
Their lawyers documented
you did think.

You were silent.
But they could see your thoughts
watching from your eyes.

You were found guilty.
They put you in jail
to empty your mind
so their thoughts could move in.

They took away your future,
then they let you go.

Released into a world of suspicion
you sent your thoughts
                                        into hiding.
You visited them secretly.
You became aware of a whole
underground of outlawed thoughts.

What is out of sight
is a difficult target.

But an empty mind attracts squatters.
They will trash your mind.

The wind comes and goes at will;
comets break away from orbiting the sun.

The future resists control.

Your thoughts are your history
your experience
part of your DNA.
Your thoughts are you.
Your ancestors live in you.

Take back your thoughts.

PUSHING BACK

Freedom is pushing back
what obstructs movement
of the spirit and the body.

A HARMONIOUS SOCIETY

The nation of a billion people
has discovered the secret
of a "harmonious society."

Many envy its success.
It's not perfect, but amazingly
good, considering the numbers.

It's a simple approach,
requiring speed and efficiency
and a team of experts.

The face of society
must have no wrinkles.
The moment a frown appears,

call in the surgeon
for reconstruction.
Cut and stretch.

It takes some pain
to get rid of a bigger pain.
Do what you must

for the sake of collective
good looks. Cripple critics,
relocate disturbers to prison

for harmony treatments
and disappear those you know
you'll never rehabilitate.

The one problem
with face-lifts is once begun
they must be continued

ad infinitum for otherwise
everything will look worse
than before the knife.

The face of this nation,
fussed over by experts, seems
at this time, wrinkle-free,

the mouth pulled back
in a permanent smile,
that often happens when

too many surgical adjustments
to arrest the evidence of time
end up distorting life.

WHAT WE DO

Struggle free is what we do

from the womb and disease,
hunger and the rain, from
blood family for the chosen
without cutting ties,

from nets cast into our minds
and repetitions that trap us
into prisons of desire,

from revered leaders
who enter without knocking
and spiritual masters
who use love to ensnare us.

CRISSCROSSING

A man raises his hand
against his brother;
one tribe enslaves another;
citizens of a powerful country
turn against each other
in war-like waves of crime;
a nation invades its neighbor;
then the tide turns
and those on top
sink to the bottom,
crosses crisscrossing,
all blood types blend,
no one immune,
no one escapes.

CERTAINTY

Freedom is skittish,
moves often,
resists certainty.

When you claim
you have it,
words will turn to stone,

houses will burn,
bridges collapse,
people will loot.

GRAY PLACE

Choosing is rejecting
— that's bullying now
definitely verboten.

You can go to jail
for not liking
people who dislike you.

No more saying No
to a stranger
demanding you share.

You can tell jokes
but only the ones
everyone finds funny.

To offend is to cause
rioting in the streets.
Lawyers will file briefs.

If you report a fire
the hoses will be turned
on the real trouble — you.

You are to follow
directions to a gray place
where no one will know you.

TRAFFIC

If you go against the traffic
maybe you know something
they don't

or it could be you're lost
and the traffic may just run
you down.

A LIFE

Office clock hands
working like thieves

recreation in shopping palls
soul-binding clothes

repetition —
another form of oblivion

checking for sanity
in distorting mirrors

pension
only a quarter century away.

SAD STORY

A man who survived years
in the guarded killing fields
of his own country
was shot to death
in the land of the free,
where success mingles
in the crowded streets.

UP TO YOU

Don't mistake freedom
for what we do with it.

The pen is not responsible
for the words written,

the knife for the surgeon's work,
the bomb for exploding.

The more power,
the greater the danger.

Freedom promises what you want
but likes to surprise you.

Freedom has its laws:
If you break them,

you must pay.
It accepts no excuses.

Everything has another face
you can't see at first.

ACID

If they throw acid in your face
for going to school,
it means the school
can give you something
to free you from the acid throwers.

CAGED

The group surrounded me,
pushed me into the cage
and snapped shut the padlock.

They watched for my reaction
and took notes as I shook
the steel bars and pleaded.

I was deprived of movement,
food I didn't like was pushed in,
they prodded and recorded.

I watched them cut open
other caged animals.
I heard their cries.

The culture doctors worked
to change life. They knew best.
They were never satisfied.

They scanned my brain
to discover how they could
cure the disease of resistance.

They were dedicated,
and kind to themselves.
They gave each other awards.

I dreamed of my dog,
open road and apples.
They made me play with keyboards.

Their screens hurt my eyes.
They wore protective goggles,
gloves and gowns.

I was naked and cold.
The cameras watched me
day and night.

When they were done,
they let me out, but
I could barely walk

and was afraid to look.
I was fitted with a gadget
to direct where I should go.

ELIZABETH I AFTER THERAPY

She refuses to leave
her spacious chambers.
She is drinking another potion
the doctors prescribed.

"I've been permanently damaged,"
Elizabeth explains.
"Look at my family.
Did I have a normal family?
Like other people? No.
A sluttish mother
and a father who was
a glutton and a murderer.

He beheaded my mother
— I was only two —
and then any person
who became fond of me.
That was his style —
torture and execution.
He left me many enemies.

And my sister: why couldn't
just one of my relatives
have been normal? A bloody
fanatic she turned out to be,

burning dissenters.
She imprisoned me
in the Tower of London.
Her timely death saved my life.

This is my inheritance.
What's the point of even trying?

If only I'd been born
into some loving peasant family,
where the father sang
as he worked in the fresh air
and my mother outlived him.

But fate had other plans.
Post-traumatic stress
is what the doctors call it,
but I say, it's not 'post' at all
but constant and will never end.
There's not a minute I'm not stressed.
Someone is always trying to kill me
to get to the throne.

Why was I put in a chair
everyone wants to sit in?

What I need is protection
from someone whose loyalty
is assured. English aristocrats
need not apply. Marriage
to a man others will fear

but who'll be grateful to me —
that rules out a French husband.
Cross Europeans off the list."

So she marries a Russian,
nephew of Ivan the Terrible.
He acts naturally,
she protests, he insists,
they shout and accuse.
She drives herself mad.
He locks her up
in a protected dungeon
and turns to rule England
into the most bloody failure.

No voyages of discovery,
no theatre, no poetry,
no song of the people.

THE AGE OF TALKERS

It's the age of talkers,
not to be confused with thinkers.
People with degrees in talking
chatting to the rest of us
busy doing other things.

It's big business — talking,
connected to buying.
You can choose the merchandise
but not the opinion.

Admire, condemn,
buy this, swallow these,
remake and update,
and don't grow old.

Agree or be accused.

They are leadership graduates,
having been taught
from age ten to say,
"I want to change the world."

It seems each generation
produces more and more people
who get paid for not growing,
cleaning, digging, building,

inventing, and looking after.
What is it about talking
that makes it more valuable
than repairing a leaking roof?

Professional talkers give off clouds
of opinions on people they don't know,
about events they did not witness.

They interview other talkers and
comment on each other's comments.
It's all about *more* and *most* —
beautiful, rich, intelligent —
to motivate you to buy.

If you don't buy, they can't lead.

The talkers talk equality
but won't share the microphone.

It's a world of noise,
colors on flat surfaces,
of dolls and toy cars,
and make-believe food.

Talkers require fans —
lots of them. They count them
regularly. High numbers
smooth out their wrinkles.

Talkers want your attention.
They act like friends.
Their smiles are disarming.
They enter your living room,
chat while you eat, drive,
and even sleep. They spend
more time with you
than you do with family.
They contact your neighbors,
colleagues and enemies.

They pretend to give you
what you want,
while they mix in a few drops
of something powerful
you can't detect.

It enters your bloodstream
to circulate their desires.
It uses your fingers to mark the X
in the deceptive ballot box.

They claim your children.
They want the future.

The words they feed you
are bleached and processed
and will not nourish you.

Their public words hide
their private actions.

But followers have their secrets too.
This makes them fickle.
Fans are not friends.
One season changes into another.
No age lasts forever.

PRISON

Each lives in some kind of prison.
The walls are not visible.
But when you try to leave,
obstruction blocks your way.

You can't see the rifles
pointed at you in the yard.
You know you've been hit
when your life collapses.

Your prison companions
share your conviction
outside has no limits,
in spite of reports from escapees.

Rumors exist: if you escape
north, south, east, or west,
you merely find yourself
in another house of correction.

Some penal resorts offer comforts:
windows without bars,
sofas, artwork, and tennis courts;
a field for riding horses.

In others, no illusions intrude
into the small spaces.
The floor is concrete cold;
the bars straight and thick.

Guards are necessary, insiders say,
to keep you from straying.
They protect from outside predators,
but mainly, from each other.

THE KEY

One can get used to anything.
There are people who live
in tight enclosures
with one barred window.

They lock themselves in
with complicated alarms
against the unexpected.

Every now and then
they parole themselves out
with the permission
of the prison guard they live with.
They keep checking the time
so they won't be late back.

They fear things going wrong.
They complain to outsiders
about their prison life
as they hurry back, the key
held tightly in their hand.

CHANGE

When saving souls
builds stone empires,
bodies get tortured.

When promises of freedom
turn into piles of laws,
thought is handcuffed.

When knowledge withdraws
into degreed institutions,
outcomes get rigged.

When curing disease
creates vast fortunes,
new diseases multiply.

When creation of new life
is replaced by dead-end
pleasures, death rules.

ENEMY

Blood does not protect;
neither do good deeds.
Your kind thoughts
won't stop the cobra.

Identified by acts that harm,
subject to change
like time and the weather
yet eternal, as light and dark.

"Love your enemies"
recognizes their existence;
otherwise, you would have
been told, "Have no enemies."

The way to have no enemy
is to obey your foe,
surrender to a hostile will
and lose your own.

When you abandon your life,
you spit on your ancestors,
forfeit your home and country,
wander lost in a foreign land.

This world always tests you
with crossroads and dead-ends.
When you face one way,
you turn your back on another.

Opposing forces rule life.
No resistance, no muscle.
The one peaceful place
on earth is the cemetery.

No point lamenting the loss
of some snakeless paradise.
Good and bad bacteria
battle for life in every body.

HATE IS A FULL-TIME JOB

Hate is a full-time job.
You must be high-energy
and dedicated to a cause.
A university degree
will open locked doors.
The right words can make
wrong disappear.

You will play it big,
gain enviable power
to decide who lives,
who dies how —
a god-like power.
You will walk on marble
and listen to praise;
people will bow
in your presence.
Enemies will confirm
your importance.

Hate energizes and arms you,
where love weakens and disarms.

It's not for everyone.
The rewards, though sensational,
are not guaranteed,
and may rebound on you
in unexpected ways.

Hate has no loyalty.
Loyalty is for the weak.
When you get in the way,
you will be taken out.
This keeps you sharp.
Promises are made to break.

Yes, it's a tough job,
                                        but
there's no end
to the applicants.

NO ESCAPE

Someone dies for our sins
all the time, but we are not saved.
The evidence against us mounts.
Forgiveness is beside the point.

There is no escape.
Our soft tissue holds us back
and the rioting in our brains
distracts our attention.

NO LIMITS

Though tied down
and walled in,
we build glass cities
above the earth,
enter each other's hearts,
play with lions,
and move among the stars.

EDUCATION

I blame the nuns.
They did a good job.
Dedicated they were;
sense of humor, too.
I still love them.

They advised no worldly
provisions on the journey.
My eyes focused up,
I ignored the down.
Why I didn't fall off a cliff

is a mystery. Love ruled.
I travelled in wild territory,
fed likeable marauders,
tried to reform the venomous.
Scars on my body

and poison in my system
reveal my strong faith.
I expected to better
but things became worse.
I still pray every day.

DON'T DO IT

I tried it.
Don't do it.

Turn the other cheek.
Now I need plastic surgery.

Don't resist evil.
Mass graves kept filling up.

Forgive the wrongdoer.
Covering up became
my full-time job.

Do good to those who hate you.
I was surprised
when the haters got better
at hating to get more good.

Give away
your worldly goods
and seek the spiritual life.
Begging for the worldly goods
of others is harder
than you think.

I tried it.
Don't do it.

MOCK EXECUTION

They tied my hands with guilt,
blindfolded me with sorrow,
stood me up against the past,
and fired their weapons.

Though injured, I didn't fall.
Dostoyevsky knew the joke.
My sentence was commuted
to exile from myself.

ONE INVITATION IS ALL YOU GET

SAFETY

This planet of refugees...
We flee from where we are
to where we think they are not,
but they are waiting for us
in our imagined place of safety.

STOP SIGN

You have been forbidden.
It is against the law.
You can be fined or jailed.

Your breath is measured:
you can take in only
so much oxygen.

If your brain is caught
trespassing, you are bled
on your way out.

Your strength is rationed
for the good of
who knows what.

You must obey the stop sign
to let civilization pass
out of sight.

WALLS

The higher the walls
the better they like it

they talk of freedom
and veil your face

they have found a system
to relieve them of thinking

they want permission
and no responsibility.

INVITATION

It's a private celebration
with a special entrance.
When I come by
you are holding
the syringe carefully,
injecting good times
into your vein.

I know you want company:
you have laid yourself out —
not in the arched doorway
shaded from view,
but on the cold pavement
swept by the street lamp.
People on their way
where you are not invited
must step into your life.
And that's your entrance
into their lives. You
curl up in a corner
of their souls and they
take you with them
wherever they go.

Your clothes are stylish:
short leather jacket
tight gray pants, black boots.
Two earrings pierce one ear.

Something about you.
Is it your confidence?
Your devotion to your desire?
Your strong belief in nothing?
Your taunt?
Or something more sinister:
an invitation.

At home, I stretch out
and turn on: old movies,
b.c. (before colour).
Dance, song and wit
enter my bloodstream.
I'm at the party:
I know the guests
but no one recognizes me.

I don't notice time passing.
Somewhere in a corner
of my soul, you nod.

It's a powerful drug
this preference for what is not
over what is.

SYMPATHY

Sympathy can inject
a drug into your vein
to make you cooperate
with what will kill you.

HOME

Born on the road
in the midst of war
I haven't stopped moving
they haven't stopped chasing
though the "they" keep changing
like fickle borders
and promises of freedom.

Wherever I am
is my home.
It fits neatly into
my travelling bag.

A rainbow arches
over the town I enter.
There is a festival going on
in the battle-scarred streets.

VANCOUVER EVENING

A quarter moon hangs
from a pale sky.
Behind the lights
of the city below,
north shore mountains
glitter for night skiers
and send greetings
across the silky night.

MARRIAGE

Something you can count on.
Nothing from the outside can break it.
Any burglary is an inside job.
Even when you consider the other
                    your worse half
no one else can criticize that half.

If you don't have it, you desire it;
when you get it, you want something else
and when you find something different,
you regret losing what you had.

It requires a periodic "I was wrong"
to keep things stable.

It can mend what is broken
and transform a cabin into a mansion.
It's a worm-aerated soil
for nourishing the future.

Though some may turn it into a long winter,
others set it up as a refuge from the cold.

POSTJUDICE

Prejudice, he said.
What you reject is in charge.
You must approve of the other.
If you refuse, you lose
your place in the line.
Who are you
to pick and choose?
You versus an army of PhDs,
MDs, and law degrees.
Nobel Prizes need no proof.
Spiritual masters know enough
to sell out concert halls.
Theories rule life.
Don't trust your experience.
Your color taints you,
your traditions condemn you.
Your laughter accuses you.
Prejudice, he said.

Post-judice, I replied.
You're assuming pre-
because you disagree.
I admit I used maps
drawn by lost travelers.
I approved of the endorsed,
derided the ridiculed.
Can't blame me entirely.
I hung around universities,

got into some bad thinking,
inhaled in libraries,
even used prizes to get high.
I avoided the marketplace.
But when consequences hit,
I saw people get sick and
communities break into pieces,
I went cold-turkey,
detoxed and scrubbed clean,
fed on ignored facts and patterns.
I accepted experience.
Postjudice, I replied.

EVERYTHING IS TEMPORARY

Change your behavior
and I'll change
my opinion of you.

Call me names
if you like;
keep adding
to your bill.

Go ahead, make
feelings a crime,
punish lack of respect,
spy on words.

I don't ask you
to pay your debts,
just to stop taking
what's left of my life.

Change your behavior
and I'll change
what I think of you.

CONFESSIONS OF A DO-GOODER

Yes, me too, when I was young.
I worked to change the world,
I mean — other people.
I signed, demonstrated, marched,
chanted and sang.
I accused and forced.
I changed laws.
I gave away money others earned.
I secretly admired
those who posed with rifles
and even a few who bombed.
Yes, I'm the university type.

Though things changed,
they remained the same.
New faces took over old roles.
A different color got the knife in the back.
Someone else always pays.
I stepped back, confused.
The more you force
the worse things become.
You have to be careful
when you open the gate
to someone seeking shelter
when behind her stand armed intruders.

NO BLAME

OK, so you do this
because your mother did that
and your father the other.
No blame attached;
you are excused.

None of this matters
as others dress their wounds
and lock their doors
against your desires
disguised as armed thieves.

VIRUS

Infectious agent
a morbid principle

can replicate only
in living hosts

colonizes, distorts
shuts down local defenses

this particular one
can spread like fire

leaving devastation
smoldering memories

no one is immune
schools breed it

churches, governments,
rogue organizers

like the Ebola,
it uses the host cell

to make copies of itself
then destroys the cell

blood will spurt
from your eyes

beware of ambitious leaders
who know what's best for you

they use your mind
to multiply themselves

you will no longer
recognize family and friends.

QUALITY

(Dedicated to those who attempt to enforce the same results on everyone.)

Equality is reassurance your neighbor
will not get too far ahead of you.

The promise is we're all one
but someone else decides which one.

Force is used to take from you
to give to others not of your choosing.

Equality invites not doing more
than others, until nothing works.

Plymouth Pilgrims lived it
into discord and starvation.

It continues to inspire. Unmarked
mass graves testify to its appeal.

Inequality is an open road.
A safe journey is not guaranteed.

No assurance is motivation
for hard work and invention.

Want and envy are harnessed
to produce what others desire.

Choice is virtue's tool:
You cannot escape responsibility.

Equality is theft.
Inequality is insecurity.

Fairness and equality
are forever estranged.

Equality or freedom. The more
you have of one, the less of the other.

CAN'T HELP IT

Forgive me, I come from a people
who can't help saying what they think.

Even after a generation or two
of punishments — long interrogations,
torture, prison, slave labor service
in icy northern regions — they still
tell you, whether you ask or not.

Relatives at family dinners,
strangers in the public market,
taxi-drivers turning round
excitedly to face the passengers
— there's no stopping us,
I'm afraid. Free or not, speech,
the genuine kind, dripping blood
or honey, will pour out.

At times we may be silent, but
I can guarantee one thing:
we will not say the naked emperor's
clothes are to die for, such elegance
and splendor, just like his mind.

IN THE DRIVER'S SEAT

I know it's ridiculous
my apologies to New Agers
teachers of the Secret
(your will commands
the Universe) but I think
I'm not in control

certainly I'm in the driver's seat
why else would I be surprised

I want to go left
all my friends went left
my life turns right
I aim to slow down
it speeds up
I try to stop
it runs a red light

haven't killed anyone yet
though I've injured a few

I step on the accelerator
it stalls in an intersection
I have it towed
then take it back

I consult and consider
I keep replacing parts

even when I reach
what I want, it's not
what I expected

I must admit moving
through the unknown
has lit my mind
and fed my heart

still, it's a mystery to me
why I'm steering in one direction
and my life is heading in another.

NOT TRUE

Everything I say
                    is not true.
It's true to some extent
and past a certain line
          — it's just a line.

The room may be too hot
or I'm winging it
or I suspect your motives
or I just want to please you.
In any case, the words

often come running out,
bypassing whoever
is working the shift
at the border. Illegals —
that's what some words are.

My aim is not to deceive —
to gain something by fraud —
but truth seems hard
to dig up, like unearthing
the roots of an old tree.

So I just break off a branch,
maybe only a discolored leaf.
Sorry about that. Words are
like rolling dice; you never
know what will turn up.

FINAL SOLUTION

I've lost faith
that taller buildings
and smaller rooms,
increased VISA credit,
out-gassing clothes,
drugs made in space,
nuclear power plants
on major earthquake faults,
other planets littered
with our spider-like gadgets,
and more efficient bombs
will save us.

No use counting on
the Nobel Prize
for the final solution.

ONE

You are handed
a set of thoughts
like a prison uniform
not your size
cut to fit another
of ideal measurements
designed for unity.

One size fits all.

We're all one.

One is just an "n"
away from none.

DON'T ASK

Can you have equality
without thought control?

Is it possible to level
without using force?
To cut down grass
without a machine
of multiple blades?

If you pretend to know
what's best for me,
can I pretend to know
how you should live?

Is there any truth in
the observation made
in the early 1800s England?

The love of liberty
is the love of others;
the love of power
is the love of ourselves.

— William Hazlitt

SILENT MOVIE

I'm in a silent movie
achingly funny
because so heartbreaking.
The written dialogue
has been removed.
The censors have provided
another set of words
but they don't fit.

The heroine says, "I love you,"
to the stranger tying her down
to the railroad tracks;
the hero thanks the posse
for shooting his father
defending his home;
the thief says, "I was robbed,"
and the prey: "I confess.
I have wounds to prove it."

The censors like it.

We in the movie
know what's going on
but the audience laughs
in all the sad places.

THE PLEDGE

Freedom is a land
not on any map,
yet we all seek it,

struggling with our chemistry,
agitated by everyone's turmoil,
friend and foe,

tripping over what we forgot
we learned — more powerful
than what we think we remember.

Sometimes a force,
five thousand miles away,
with the momentum of almost
two thousand years,
joins present discontents
to create a storm
heading our way.

The only chance we may have
is a pledge of loyalty
to something that exists
only in the imagination.

If

If you think you're free
the walls will close in.

If you think there's nothing
on the other side
you won't bother to look.

To move through and out
it helps to learn
to see in the dark.

When shapes are distorted
survival may mean
factoring in the distortion.

If you don't get off
the road leading to nowhere
before you get there
the road back will disappear

or maybe not, but
you will no longer see it
due to failing vision.

Of course, some say
all roads lead to nowhere.
There may be truth in it,

but not enough to ignore
that other routes will
create different memories.

If you keep moving
toward the light
                    it may reveal
what you're stepping on
and what is within reach.

OFF ENDS

He who laughs at an offense
off-balances the offender
and ends the offense.

LIGHT

The setting sun burns white
in the smoky sky,
streaming light into the bay,
over restless water,

on a path toward anyone
along the water's edge;
a silver trail through
a graying evening.

If you move, the path of light
follows you. If you stop,
it waits for you like a pet dog
used to your routines.

None of us can see the light
the other is receiving;
each is a planet around
which the sun revolves.

BEWARE

Beware of doing well
I mean really well
standing alone.

I'm not saying don't,
merely: expect everything.

After praises and prizes
may come punishment.

Kisses can carry poison.

Remember Yakovlev
16th century architect
of St. Basil's Cathedral
for Ivan the Terrible.

A legend claims
Ivan had him blinded
so he would never again
build anything so beautiful.

Whether it happened or not
the legend is true.

RESTLESS

We are a restless tribe
that needs to move,
across waters and deserts,
down into the earth
looking for our past,
out to distant planets
to make a new start,
back and forth in time,
changing our homes,
building into the sky,
crossing fears,
flying without wings,
killing what we value,
rescuing what we injure,
blinded by beauty,
waging war on pain,
snatching the divine
from time.

RING OF FIRE

(Dedicated to the Japanese people,
March 2011)

I live in the Ring of Fire.
There's a fault line close by.
It goes under the sea
to a nearby Island.
We are aware the earth
under us can shift
its connections any time
and we may have to start
all over again.

I used to live right on
a major fault line in California.
Anxiety line. Periodic predictions
of the city by the sea
                    collapsing
woke us from dreams
of safe houses
and secret gardens.

Now I watch on the screen
my neighbors across the Pacific
in the same Ring of Fire
be shocked once again
into the nature of this planet.

The sea sends a wave
10 meters high, at jet speed

— 500 miles an hour —
to do what the 9 quake left undone.
It engulfs the northeast coast,
destroying farmlands,
swirling through town streets,
picking up boats, cars, trucks,
parked planes to smash
whatever blocks its way.
It rips a child from
the mother's arms,
drowns old people trapped
in their homes. It takes
motorists for a death ride.

They are picking up a thousand
bodies the sea is returning
to the catastrophe coast
where six nuclear reactors
in the same compound
are exploding and burning.

Stricken with loss, the people
are looking after each other,
sharing what they have.
They are in shock, grieving,
but calm and already picking
up the debris and clearing.
They are family.
They are rearranging bonds.

The nature of this planet,
beautiful and faulty,
with its seasonal patterns
and unpredictable instability,
like us, with our fault lines
in our genes, our families,
cultures and dreams, facing
historical forces shifting
their own tectonic plates
without warning, or perhaps
we just don't know
how to read the signals.

We all live in a Ring of Fire.
Fault lines cross our lives.
Strong bonds are a lifeline.

THE CHOSEN

To be born is to be chosen.
— John O'Donohue
A Book of Celtic Wisdom

If the two carriers of history —
millions of years of selecting,
dodging death and passing on DNA
— if they had not crossed paths
if she had not placed
the newspaper ad
or he had not read it

if one wrong word
a stranger's smile of interest
a song from another land
had diverted the gaze
of either one

even in their union
you had only a day or so
out of forever
to enter this life

the ambitious sperm
that carried half of you
had to run an obstacle course
before uniting with the other half
encased in protective walls
millions of other sperm

were pushing their own half
but only one, if any, was going
to penetrate the bridal egg
fusing the two halves
into a chosen

it was winner take all
a race against time
before the egg died
or the sperm succumbed
along the way

yes, if just one event
in a million
had not happened
you would have missed
your chance

so, please, no more
trips to the past to prevent
your father marrying your mother
no wishing she had chosen
a rich man
no desire for designer genes
no retelling the story
to give yourself royal blood
and vast fortune

no using your allotted time
to rebirth yourself
on another planet

without war or work
only kindly neighbors
who plant flowers in your yard

where merchandise is free
and the weather — beach
all year round
and everyone admires
your religion
agrees with your politics
and wants to hear your opinion.

One invitation is all you get.

EVERYDAY THINGS

If everything is sacred
you will use the knife carefully.

The meal you will place on the table
will nourish more than the body.

The vow you take to serve
will turn sacrifice to pleasure.

If all things carry meaning
you will let pain heal.

No matter if your home is one room
you will place a flower to greet the light.

If blessings often come disguised, you
will take home the thin dog with the sad eyes.

A TOAST

To bonds
we're born into
those we make
the ones we resist;

to obstacles
that test our desire
develop courage
point the way;

to the unknown
where we send
fragments of our lives
to seed flowers of light.

TRAVEL ADVICE

Leave behind
what you don't want
in your future.

Pack only
what will not obstruct
your movement.

Take a change
of preferences.

Include some items
to give away.

Learn the rules
of where you're going.

Watch out for
what you don't expect.

Keep on good terms
with the angel sent
to accompany you.

A CHANCE

Here's a garden.
You can call it Eden.

It will have the best
and the worst.

Your chemistry will
match it perfectly.

That should make things
interesting. Busy too.

See what you can make
of it. I'm done.

ACKNOWLEDGMENTS

Some of the poems were published online in Jonathon Narvey's www.propagandistmag.com and Butler Shaffer's column, "A Poet Speaks of Liberty," at www.lewrockwell.com.

The Czeslaw Milosz's quote comes from "Ars Poetica?" in *Bells In Winter,* The Ecco Press, New York, 1978.

John O'Donohue's quote comes from *Anam Cara, A Book of Celtic Wisdom*, p. 83, HarperCollins Publishers, 1997.

My deep gratitude to my sister, Laima Vian, for her steadfast anti-sentimentality treatments (any sentimentality still to be found in my work is entirely my fault); to my linguist cousin, Giedre Bufiene, for her thoughts; to Professor Ron Dart for his unfailing good will and endeavor to bring out the best in me; to Professor Walter Block, who said, "Don't stop," when I kept emailing him my work; to Dan Rusen for his generous comments; to fellow poets Bernice Lever, Lucia Gorea and Daniela Elza; and to the gracious Jane Shaffer.

I owe much to college economics instructor Paul Geddes and his libertarian group, whose lively discussions over the years helped me to think more deeply about freedom.

I'm indebted to my wonderful neighbors, Don and Jo Ann Dyck, who organized neighborhood poetry meetings so I could get uncensored feedback; and to Dale and Donna Leibel, who conveniently live across the street, for their literary opinions and for Dale's unfailing computer rescues.

CPSIA information can be obtained at www.ICGtesting.com
Printed in the USA
BVOW011054170212

283180BV00001B/2/P